Like a Shadow The Night
Poems of love, loss and consolation

by

Maggie Shaw

Like a Shadow The Night
Poems of love, loss and consolation

by

Maggie Shaw

eregendal.com

Also by the Author
The Vision and Beyond (2018)
Diviner's Nemesis I – Avenger (2019)
Diviner's Nemesis II – Retribution (2020)
The Eagle and The Butterfly (2020)
The Last Thursday Ritual in Little Piddlington (2021)
The Eagle and The Raven (2021)
Waiting for the Dawn (2022)
The Teddies of Rosehill Cottage (2022)
The Eagle and The Hart (2022)

First published in the United Kingdom in 2023 by
Eregendal.com, Rosehill Road, Crewe, Cheshire, CW2 8AR.
Printed in the United Kingdom by University College Chester.

Copyright © 2023 Maggie Shaw

The contents of this book convey the thoughts of the author at the time of writing and may not necessarily represent the author's present point of view.

All rights reserved. No part of this publication may be reproduced, stored in a retrieval system, or transmitted, in any form or by any means, electronic, mechanical, photocopying, recording or otherwise, without the prior permission of the publisher and copyright holder; except in the case of brief quotations embodied in critical reviews and certain other non-commercial uses permitted by copyright law.

ISBN 978-1-7397801-5-9 (paperback)

Contents

Introduction and Acknowledgements   vii

Love   9

Life   25

Depression   41

Faith and Recovery   57

Stories   73

People and Places   93

Humour   113

About the Author   123

Index of Poems   124

Introduction and Acknowledgements

Like A Shadow, The Night is my second collection of poems written over the course of my lifetime. The poems naturally fell into the sections presented in this book as I put the collection together.

The poetry charts my progression from a teenage runaway in London, my recovery from severe clinical depression through the Twelve Step Program, the emotional transformation of a late diagnosis of Autistic Spectrum Disorder, and a wonderful time of creativity as I enter my final decades. The poems are not in chronological order. Recovery, as someone first told me in my late twenties, is not a straight diagonal line from zero to 100% on the graph of life. Rather, it happens in a series of waves, with each peak usually a little higher than the previous one, and each dip usually not quite as deep.

Many people have helped me in the different stages of my life, through depression, addiction, recovery, diagnosis, education and publishing: too many to mention in person. I try to repay my debt to those people by supporting others the way they supported me.

As always, I would like to thank those who helped with the book in any way, including Wendy Peacock for her guidance, Ernie Jones Jnr for his poem overleaf about my church work, and all who took part in the vote for the cover design. The photos used in the cover and illustrations were sourced through a Pro subscription to www.canva.com.

A special mention must go to my late musical partner in crime, Roy Butler, who sadly passed away just four months before I put the final touches to this collection. Roy was always a great encourager, and we miss him very much.

Any faults in the work are my own alone.

Maggie Shaw, 14th March 2022

There was a young lady from Asparagus
Who thought the world of all of us.
She played the organ with Augustus
September, October, November, December, exceterus
And she also fed the lot of us.
Souper Woman!!!!
        E.J.jnr

Section One

Love

The love poem *For All Eternity* describes the hopes and fears of Liz Kirkland and Alec Graham, as they got married in the early pages of *Diviner's Nemesis I – Avenger*. The flaws in their characters meant they would have to sacrifice a lot to find their happy ending after their fairytale wedding.

A recording of this poem as a song is available at www.eregendal.coem/music and other online stores.

For All Eternity   1980s

I have loved you, my love, since we met;
I have loved you before all time.
I have loved you in body, and loved you in soul:
I have yearned for this day when you'd be mine.

I'll love you forever, though the stars leave the sky;
I'll love you, though time ceases to be;
I'll love you forever, though the sun cools and dies:
I will love you for all eternity.

You are all I have dreamed you would be;
You are all I have sought in a man:
You complete my existence, you fill my desire;
You have saved me from drowning in life's storm.

I'll love you forever, though the stars leave the sky;
I'll love you, though time ceases to be;
I'll love you forever, though the sun cools and dies:
I will love you for all eternity.

I have nothing in life to regret
Because all of my past leads to you.
You have given me hope in a world of despair,
And a life that is radiant and new.

I'll love you forever, though the stars leave the sky;
I'll love you, though time ceases to be;
I'll love you forever, though the sun cools and dies:
I will love you for all eternity.

My Love   22nd November 1977

My love has fine long blond hair,
Blood-red lips, and eyes of blue.
My love never seems to care
For things that trouble me and you.

My love dresses like a scruff
But looks like a noble queen.
My love laughs when things get rough:
She would never make a scene.

My love dances in the rain;
She plays snowballs in the snow.
My love soothes away my pain,
Makes even its memory go.

My love cheers me when I cry,
Bucks me up when things go wrong;
My love eases my soul's sigh;
So to her I sing this song.

My love lies and dreams with me,
As we watch our castles grow.
But we two cannot be free –
We cannot let the hard world know.

    Unable to concentrate enough to embark upon a novel during her long hospital stay in 1977, Maggie channelled her creativity into writing scenes and poems like snapshots of characters who would find their way into the novels she wrote in the years that followed. This is one such poem.

Just Say The Word   **2nd July 1990**

Remember the time we spent
On our first day together.
Remember the fun we had
In all that sunny weather.
If you do recall
And you would still like me to call,
Just say the word, and I'll come round
And we can fall in love.

There are so many things
I'd love to tell and show you.
There are so many places
I could get to know you.
If you'd like to come
And you would like to join the fun,
Just say the word, and I'll come round
And we can fall in love.

This song evokes the easy listening pop culture of the 1960s. The songs topping the charts of that era often had an innocence about love and relationships, which more modern pop songs now often lack. Here, the singer recalls a lost opportunity to date someone in times gone by, and invites them to take the chance of finding love if they would like to.

    Maggie often writes circular poems and stories. This early *Love Song* describes an imaginary past relationship in the familiar places know to the poet at the time she wrote the piece. Her teenage dreams of finding romance in companionship never quite came true until many years later.

Love Song   Summer 1971

… And the wind blew gently through the grass,
Through the ashes,
Through his hair.

Across the lake we sailed,
Birds calling,
Helm dipping;
And his eyes were always in mine;
And my words drifted gently across the water,
Across the night.

By the beck we strolled,
Grass waving,
Water singing;
And his thoughts were always with mine;
And my smile shone through the darkness,
Through the night.

Through the streets we drove,
Window shopping,
Christians preaching;
And his hand was always in mine;
And my happiness glowed around us,
About our path.

By the fire we sat,
Embers glowing,
Darkness gath'ring;
And our love always burning strong;
And the wind blew gently through the grass,
Through the ashes,
Through his hair…

Maggie wrote *To Dying Love* about four months before she separated from her first husband, Bob. She was working for the Citizens Advice Bureau at the time. The irony of her situation made it feel all the more poignant. She could see the problems she faced but did not know how to resolve them.

To Dying Love   14th May 1977

Who will advise the advisors
When they want to cry?
Who will save the saviours
When they have to die?
Who will help the heroes
When they don't know what to do?
Who can help me?
And who can help you?

For you were my advisor
In the night,
And you were my saviour,
Giving light;
And you were my hero,
Helping me get through:
Once, what you were to me,
I was to you.

Who will teach the teacher,
Now we've new things to learn?
And who will love the lover
Now that hate's flames burn?
And which of us has got the sword
Which now cuts us apart?
And who can find the salve
To ease this hardening heart?

Pattern is an evocative poem describing the creeping awareness that a relationship is dead, through the medium of image perspective. The tension builds the closer to the object the imagery moves.

This is an autistic perception of emotion: seen in layers of dawning revelation over time. It is not that an autist has no emotions, more that it takes time for an autist to process those emotions. Indeed, many autists like the poet, feel emotions very deeply and powerfully indeed.

Pattern   10th September 1974

Pattern dappled low beneath my blistered feet
I look down from above, but before we meet,
Across the horizon a river flows by:
Goodbye.

Ashes drift about my being, touch my eyes.
I speak to answer the mountain's distant cries.
Across the horizon a boat sails by:
Goodbye.

Clouds of misty ochre reach about my hair.
I touch their cold fronds and find I stand no-where.
Across the horizon a man walks by:
Goodbye.

Wreaths of psychedelic flowers bloom around.
I shout with tears in my eyes but hear no sound.
Across the horizon a face laughs by:
Goodbye.

Chiffon scarves of night entwine about my limbs.
I scream in silence as emptiness begins.
Across the horizon an eye sneers by:
Goodbye.

Images shatter, patterns smash, memories begin.
How much time must pass before I look again?
Across the horizon, out of my life, he walked away.
Goodbyes are so lonely – I just said, 'Okay'.

Where is the scheme   July 1977

Where is the scheme, the yesterday dream
That others promised to show?
Where is the one, that special sun
They said would chase away the snow?

Oh, I know, life is just how you make it,
But my hands can't create any more;
And I know, life is just how you take it,
But I can't steal any more.

When I met you, love made me new:
You stayed, and with you came the day.
Now you have gone, and I'm all alone.
Now nothing can chase the blues away.

For I know, life is just how you make it,
But my hands can't create any more;
And I know, life is just how you take it,
But I can't steal any more.

After the break-up of a relationship, both the people involved take time to recover. This poem expresses some imagery from that period of mourning for all that has been lost, that time of bargaining and helplessness. Logic no longer controls thoughts and actions as more instinctive reactions take over the hurt mind.

How I Miss You 1975

You have gone, but here I stay.
How I miss you every day:
Every day I feel so blue.
Please come back –
I still love you.

You were hurt cos I was cruel.
Now I know I was the fool:
Was the fool to be untrue.
Please come back –
I still need you.

You were right and I was wrong.
Now every night for you I long.
With you I long to start anew.
Please come back –
I still want you.

Now alone each night I cry,
Wishing you hadn't said goodbye,
Said goodbye to all we knew.
Please come back –
Oh, how I miss you.

Maggie included the extra syllable in the last line of this poem despite the break in meter, to express the depth of hurt from the loss.

A song recording of *How I Miss You* can be found at www.eregendal.com/music.

The song *Look On and Laugh* expresses the venom of a woman scorned. The piece is vengeful rather than romantic. How sad that love can come to this – but was it really love in the first place?

Look on and Laugh   20th February 1977

The ferry sails the morning tide,
The seagulls swoop the valleys wide
And Death shall take his fearful bride
While I look on and laugh.

The sunset daubs the racing sea.
The judge is jailed, the guilty freed;
For you were judge who condemned me,
While I looked on and laughed.

For you first taught me how to cry,
And then you forced me on to die,
But from my ashes arose – I –
While I looked on and laughed.

I laughed at you and burnt your hide,
Like you, ignored the tears you cried,
Then stole the things that you denied,
While I looked on and laughed.

Goodbye, fellow, won't you say
Goodbye?
It's been nice knowing you. Won't you say
It's been nice knowing you!

Section Two

Life

Maggie wrote *When I* as an exercise during the Nottingham Beyond The Spectrum online writing course for neurodivergent people, which she attended via Zoom in 2021. She enjoyed the challenge of describing two things that energised her and two things that sapped her energy. The poem helped her understand why she behaved the way she did in some stressful situations. It also revealed that being with other people did not always make her feel drained: the circumstances and her autonomy influenced whether she felt secure or overwhelmed in a particular situation.

When I…   13th April 2021

When I perform music – singing and playing
Alone or with my friends or my band,
I want the moments to last forever.
I feel elated, gifted, transformed
Into a different place, a brave new world.

When I'm in my office, taking phone calls,
Hearing people make decisions about my time,
I feel trapped and resentful because
I didn't sign up for this: I didn't say yes.
I want to shout and scream profanities
And jump on the spot to vent my anger.

When I talk in a group of like-minded friends
And the conversation inspires
With talk of truth and honesty and justice,
I want to stay in that group forever.
I feel energised and taken to new heights.

When I face meeting after meeting,
And people are not honest, or they accuse me,
Or fire questions at me when I have no strength to answer,
I want to run away and hide and cower and cry.
I feel helpless and my mind goes blank.

When I walk the fells or by the sea
Or in a wood, or country place alone,
I feel the trees and hills embracing me.
The sea and skies envelop me in love.
I want to stay in that loving haven forever,
For there I sense the touch of my God.

Numbers was a poem which surprised the poet as she wrote it. It starts off as a protest against the injustices in the world, but the last line transforms it into something quite different. This is the magic of creative inspiration: as a writer, one may start the process, but sometimes the muse takes over and touches the creation with a magic wand, sending it in a new, unplanned direction.

Numbers   9th November 1974

Numbers
Lots of numbers
Few numbers

Millions – starving
Thousands – feeling
Hundreds – praying
Tens – giving

Millions – poor
Thousands – well off
Hundreds – rich
Tens – so stinking rich
    they don't know what to do with even the interest

Millions – crying
Thousands – smiling
Hundreds – laughing
Tens – too wrapped up in themselves to care

Many doing
Few seeing
Many talking
Few hearing
Many hurting
Few healing

I cannot be alone.

The poem *Just four more little months* was written towards the end of a very difficult two years for the poet, which began when Maggie fled to a Woman's Aid Refuge during her time reading Divinity at Edinburgh University. She studied during the day and became a support worker in the evenings to pay her way, while fighting a challenging divorce at the same time. The four-month period referred to was the target of finishing her final exams, which would free her to live and work anywhere she chose.

Just four more little months   18th February 2001

I just have to hold on –
See the white-ridged knuckles,
The tense and strained expression –
Only four more little months.

How wonderful to get that voice back again –
The break-through price just sorrow,
The scream lying frozen in the throat:
Where were you hiding, little girl in this woman?

So much time lost, oh, how long!
Just four more little months –
But they are eternities
After the years of the locusts.

Dear God, help me to hold on –
I am so near the summit of the mountain:
A few more steps, a little more resolve;
But I am so exhausted…

Only four more little months;
And oh, then the vista below my stumbling feet!
Here, I offer the future the pledge born of the past –
That resurrected past drawn from my marrow.

It sure is a hard world, man, but...   6th April 1972

Look, man,
No-one's gonna blow your bugle:
They don't want your germs.

No-one's gonna build your bridges –
You are your own construction gang.

An' no-one's gonna cry your tears,
So you'd better dry your eyes quick.

Out there in the wilds of the city
It's a free for all,
And the best man wins;
So at the end,

No-one's gonna reap your crop.
You've got your own barns to store it in.

    This poem reflects the language and idiom of the people the poet mixed with during her late teenage years in the early 1970s. It promises that the need for self-reliance in life's struggles can bring about a positive conclusion in the end.
    Maggie wrote the poem a month after returning home from living in London as a teenage runaway. It voices the hope she had then that things would improve.

The Night Watchman   September 1973

Go to sleep, pleasant dreams:
The Night Watchman guards over you –
Through the window, across the sky,
He's there watching, till the morning dew.

So don't you worry if the night is long,
Because he's there, child, keeping you safe;
And if you get lonely, he's there by your side;
He's always there, dear, if you keep faith.

Those seven stars, dear, so high in the sky:
They're the Night Watchman; and he guards the night long,
Until you awake for another new day,
In mother's arms where you belong.

The image of the constellation *The Night Watchman* reassuring the child of being kept safely through the night, was one Maggie returned to again and again, and rewrote several times. It reflects the sort of motherly care she did not receive because of the 1950s fashion in child rearing called Healthy Neglect. Can neglect ever be healthy?

The constellation itself does not exist, except in the writer's imagination. She wrote a lot of science fiction at that time, and the constellation was part of that world building.

    As a teenager, Maggie was ardently anti-war, and she is still a pacifist, but not a passivist, which many people seem to think is the same.

    This poem decries warfare and observes how the warmongers are not usually the people who suffer from the damage and privations of armed conflict.

Why Cry 'Blood'? Summer 1972

Gun shots,
Enemy hatred,
People mourning –
This is the meaning of war.

Exploding shells,
Alien humans,
Death –
This is the meaning of war.

The drone of aircraft,
Fear in the night,
People eternally alone –
This is the meaning of war.

The bloody battlefield,
The hostility,
The despair –
This is the meaning of war.

The empty street,
The crumbling house,
The starving, lonely child –
This is the meaning of war.

So you,
And you, and you,
Why cry for the blood of other men
When it is your own that will fall?
Oh yes, for me,
This is the meaning of war.

    Now We Rest is a corollary to the preceding poem, observing how all our achievements end in death. Whether we are powerful or poor, we all suffer the same eventual fate.
    Maggie wrote the poem as a reflection about Remembrance Day during her four months' hospital stay in 1977.

Now We Rest 6th November 1977

Now we rest –
We who have conquered mountains,
We who have fought with monsters
And won –
Now we rest.

Now we sleep –
We who levelled monuments,
We who raised up monoliths
Which stand –
Now we sleep.

Now we wait –
We who struck down nations,
We who grappled with the world
And ruled –
Now we wait.

Now we die –
We who dreamed of empires,
We who schemed for kingdoms
And laughed –
Now we die.

Now we rest –
We who were fashioned from dust,
We who were but a breath,
A leaf –
Now we rest.

There is a timelessness in *The Last Song* that goes beyond the noise and chatter of every day. It is as if the poet tuned into the background music of the universe and heard the song of creation.

The Last Song 30th March 1975

Time stops –
As though invisible wings, arrested,
Hang suspended, impatient,
In a song.

Life stops –
As though by some irresistible bond
Which overcame its prison
In the song.

Thought stops –
As though an eternal chord, striking deep,
Struck too deep, and ceased to be
In the song.

Earth stops
And waits, attendant, on the final notes
Whose harmony will never die;
Nor will the song.

Section Three

Depression

If the poems in this section speak so deeply to you that they take you back into the deep mineshaft of depression, please try to seek help. Lives can be transformed, just as the poet's life eventually was, through the help of supportive, non-judgemental people.

Starshine   1971

Starshine,
Glinting in my window,
Can I find
The things I want to know?

Sunset,
Reddening the fir tree,
Can I get
What is so dear to me?

Moonglow,
Silvering the hilltop,
Can I know,
Or do I always have to hope?

Rainstorm,
Filling up the lake,
Can I have
The things I long to take?

Whispers
In my mind at dawn,
Fill me
And make my heart forlorn.

Starshine is a haunting song about teenage doubt and striving. Teenagers often seem over-confident and brash, but many are struggling behind that front, ill-equipped to understand the world in which they are becoming adults.

Fly Away 13 November 1972

Fly away,
Fly away on the wind
To that land of beauty
Miles from where I lie.

Fly away,
Fly away, saddened mind,
To that land of beauty
Where the wild birds fly.

Fly away,
Fly away to your kind
In that land of beauty:
Don't let chance pass by.

Fly away,
Fly away: try to find
In that land of beauty,
Half the tears I cry.

Fly away,
Fly away, and unbind
Those memories of beauty
That you never should have known.

Fly Away describes the desire to escape from the worry and guilt that make up such a large part of depression. It is so difficult to share such emotions, but finding a way to do so can be the first step to overcoming them.

Black Candle is an evocative poem about writer's block which Maggie wrote in her teens. The irony of the poem is that though she feared never to write again, the very act of writing the poem shows she had overcome that block.

Black Candle   Winter 1970-71

Black candle, black candle,
Give me the shadow on the window;
Black candle, black candle,
Show me your reflection on the wall.

Across the stormy pathways of the years
I stumbled,
Hunting for the peace and seclusion of four walls,
Longing to see your golden light again.

Red willow, red willow,
Shelter me from the night song;
Red willow, red willow,
Call my words across the dark.

Through the mountains of the hours
I climbed,
Praying to find a place with a roof for my bed,
Hoping to see your boughs in the sunshine.

Flying pen, flying pen,
Trace your silver words across the page;
Flying pen, flying pen,
Put them in neon on the city walls.

Between the rocks of every second
I struggled,
Trying to find a place to rest my heart,
Praying to be able to use you again.

Like a Shadow, the Night is an evocative poem about disappointment. At the time the poet wrote it, she was running a successful start-up business which her colleagues were plotting to steal. They succeeded.

Like a shadow, the night 25th October 1987

Like a shadow, the night:
The night that holds such sorrows
In the dark folds of its cloak.

Present vision of the past
Can make the past lie;
But only by recalling the past
Can the present gain perspective.

The child stands so small against the mountain,
Insignificant against the storm:
A single flame in the darkness.

Yet a child will be the man
Who influences nations
And commands millions
And rapes the world of her store.

A child was the man who saved the world,
Who fought the world and lost,
Who wrestled with number and understood creation.

And I who as a child
Wanted to influence the world,
I cannot even influence myself
Or control my own affairs.

Others succeed now where I failed:
O, how I feel my failure,
Though I still struggle to succeed in something new.

Like a shadow, the night:
The night that holds such dreams,
And then withholds them in its cloak.

To my psychiatrist   30th June 1975

He did not see the sadness
In my heart
He did not hear the sighing
On my part

And I, I just sat there and laughed
And I, I just sat there and cried.

Days laughter echoes through the empty chimney pots in clouds of rain as winds bemuse the moaning artichokes of Sybil's lament which died sadly on that awful day when we were glad.

He did not see the fear
In my eyes
He did not hear the tears
My soul cries

And I, I just sat there and laughed
And I, I just sat there and cried.

Soubriquet darling on your silver pedestal you light your lamp, flicking cigarette ash from your golden holder that strikes through the air like a silver sword – you never even read the Times Literary Supplement to hear of his death. For he is gone, and I, I am no-one, not because he's gone, but because he was someone.

He did not see the truth
That I said
He did not hear the secrets
In my head.

And I, I just sat there laughing
And I, I just sat there crying.

He does not know the emptiness of looking into aeons and seeing the path to travel, he does not see that those future aeons are painted like the past – in black.

He did not see me
Though I was there
He did not hear me
In my despair

And I, I just sat there laughing
And I, I just sat there crying.

This sad poem describes the complete disconnect Maggie felt when first seen by an NHS psychiatrist to treat her depression.

The consultant opened the meeting by asking what she wanted him to do for her. As an autistic person, she had no idea how to reply to such a direct question and just stayed silent. She recalled little else of the meeting, except that he prescribed different antidepressants, which caused severe side effects. She didn't see him again, only his registrars. The second antidepressants prescribed by the department were so ineffective, she tried to commit suicide by overdosing on them.

She started the long journey to recovery with the support of friends, and through writing her novel *The Eagle and The Butterfly* in the long hot summer of 1976.

The Unseen Castle 20th July 1976

When I was a child, I had a house
I'd made myself from leaves and branches.
It was my castle, my refuge: the place
Where many fierce battles of ancient times were fought.
There beneath the pine trees in the old wood
So many wars were won and lost, so much blood shed,
That I could hear the ghosts' cries in the night.
But I was safe from the ghosts because
It was my castle, and in my kingdom.

One day, someone visited my castle.
I was pleased to see him; welcomed him,
For he was one whom I loved and who loved me.
I showed him round my castle and my grounds,
Gave him permission to wander there alone.
He looked at the branches, the leaves, the small wood,
And laughed.

When he saw how hurt I was, he apologised
And inspected everything again.
I was more cautious this time, of course,
But gradually felt that he could see my kingdom,
And did appreciate my castle;
Until he trod on it.

He wondered why he and I felt estranged.
I knew that though one loves, one needn't understand,
But still, I had expected some respect.
As I did not get any for my castle, I hid away,
Locking myself inside, till finally I repented and came out.
By now, my castle was all that was dear,
And so I set about repairing it after the storms
Which had raged outside while I cowered alone.

He chopped down a tree
Which landed on top of my castle,
Crushing it.
And he did not even realise.

This poem describes the poet's relationship with her father, who could not understand her emotional problems as a child.

In 1969, when she was fourteen, Maggie realised she was mentally ill and reached out to her father for help. She had seen an American film about a schizophrenic woman who had recovered with the right treatment, which gave her hope. Unfortunately, when she used it as a vehicle to ask for help, her father dismissed the film, saying it was just another Hollywood happy ending – people don't get better like that in real life.

Maggie did not ask for help again for several years. There were many suicide attempts, and two attempts to run away from home, the second of which was successful.

As an adult, it is easy to see Maggie should have reached out to someone else when her first attempt had failed. But her hope had been crushed. She believed she could never recover, that she was doomed to be mentally ill for the rest of her life. Ten years later, her doctor confirmed that diagnosis.

But by the grace of God and through a recovery fellowship, she lived to prove those predictions wrong.

So if you find yourself in a similar situation now, please reach out again, to someone you can trust and who you believe will listen. It's never too late to begin recovery, and no mental illness is too deep for the right treatments to help bring improvement.

Circles   **12th January 1976**

In what desperate circles do we swim?
What hopes to lose, treasures to win?
And what will end what we begin?

In what desperate circles do we run?
What night to flee, towards what sun?
And what regrets for what's begun?

In what desperate circles do we turn?
What dreams to love, what fears to spurn,
And what in that time will we learn?

In what desperate circles do we twist?
What hand the palm, what hand the fist,
And what is gained for what is missed?

In what desperate circles do we play!
What makes our night, what makes our day!
And what is ne'er gambled away?

Untitled   **12th December 1977**

What death it is
To dream of being free,
And then to wake up
Alone, lying here.

When it's all over   February 1974

When it's all over, at the end of the day,
You can only think of the memories before they all fade away,
And wonder if it's worth the time and the care
That took you from the moment you were born
                              to where you are.

People say it's wrong to run away from life;
But people are often wrong, and when you ran
                              you did find some relief,
And in running, you escaped the need for help,
For in that deed, you found you could still be true to yourself.

Now you know that life must end where it began.
The wheel of fortune spins, holding good and bad
                              balanced in your life span.
The circle always finishes, the lines always meet –
It's up to you not to fall, and accept fate in defeat.

Faces lie before me, smiling through the years,
And as I look, behind their faded eyes and on their cheeks
                              I see tears.
They have travelled further: they have gone before.
I pass my time with memories, till I see them once more.

Maggie wrote the poem *When it's all over* when she was eighteen, imagining how she would think at the end of her life about her choice as a teenager to run away from home and live in London for two years.

'Twixt Sky and Sod 15th July 1976

Maggie sat in another chair
While I sat and watched her ruffle her hair,
All the while wondering where we were.
'Twixt sky and sod we hung.

Maggie thought in another way
While I sat and thought on the passing day
And all night's sodden ashes decayed –
'Twixt sky and sod they hung.

Maggie dreamed in another world
While I sat and saw the hate that was hurled,
And all the endless pain it incurred:
'Twixt sky and sod it ran.

Maggie hoped in another dream
While I sat and saw through all she had seen
Because nothing was quite what it had seemed –
'Twixt sky and sod we ran.

Maggie and I, another one
Who together through hell and heaven ran,
Found only the night though we sought the sun –
'Twixt sky and sod we died.

The third person approach in this poem expresses a depersonalisation sometimes found in people who are deeply depressed.

The aftermath of sorrow 18th March 1982

I feel numbed –
Self-anaesthetised
By emotional exhaustion.
Sore eyes, no longer red,
Struggle dryly to stay open.
An aching body senseless
After the uncontrollable tremors
Have ceased.

The storm has ended.

A dull twilight peace
Pervades the silent landscape.
The lonely silhouette tops the hill
To gaze with unseeing eyes
To the emptied horizon
And beyond.

Night steals in through the window.

The darkness is still there:
The lamp cannot bring respite
To the farther corners;
Nor is the pain finished
When the break is not mended,
The amputation not healed.

Do not trust tomorrow.

The sun is not certain to rise.
It may for others, but might not for me.
I need to find an inner light
But know not what to look for
Or where or how…
Or why.

Section Four

Faith and Recovery

Selah is a Hebrew word found in the Psalms, thought by some to be an instruction to insert a break in singing; by others to mean 'forever'. The word is also used as a Hebrew personal name meaning 'to praise' or 'to pause and reflect upon what has just been said'. This last interpretation fits the context of this poem most closely.

Selah, Selah   19th November 1975

In this world you are no slave;
Selah, selah, be brave;
Oh, pray, for still one comes to save.

In this world you are no pawn;
Selah, selah, brave scorn;
Oh pray, for soon will come that morn.

In this world you can be free;
Selah, selah, wait, see;
Oh, pray, for one day you will be.

In this world you can be true;
Selah, selah, those few...
Oh pray for them to be with you.

In this world you still can live;
Selah, selah, so give;
Oh pray for those who still believe.

In this world you can still be;
Selah, selah, aye see;
Oh pray for help, and pray for me.

Prisoner   **22ⁿᵈ November 1977**

Bars.
See the bars.
Lord God, set me free.

Caged:
Padlocked cage.
Lord God, set me free.

Locks,
Rusted locks.
Lord God, set me free.

Hope?
Where's my hope?
Lord God, set me free.

Maggie was about half-way through a long hospital stay when she wrote *Prisoner*. The hardest thing can be to wait, which she had to do for nearly four months as her injuries healed and she lost more and more weight.

She never lost her belief in God, though sometimes she doubted her faith and struggled with her circumstances.

She came to discover that whenever she stopped belonging to a faith community, her depression worsened. The support and fellowship of other believers, and the Christian message carried by them, always had a beneficial effect on her life, particularly on her mental health.

Raise your glass   28th November 1977

Raise your class to memories, kid.
Cheers to the times we laughed.
The past was a bitter pill, kid:
A nasty taste you cannot wash away.

So raise your glass to the present, kid.
Cheers to the times we laugh.
The present is an uphill climb, kid:
It's not easy in these bitter gales.

So raise your glass to the future, kid.
Cheers to the times we'll laugh.
The future's looking pretty grim, kid;
But it's the only way that we can go.

Raise Your Glass was written just a few days after the preceding poem. There is a resignation and acceptance which shows Maggie's development of thought during that long hospital stay.

One of the healthiest ways to live is to accept life on life's terms. That means accepting things one cannot change, like the weather and how other people think and act. If a situation is not to our liking, we should try to alter the things we can change, either to withdraw from the situation or to change our attitude towards it.

Maggie's only way to escape the confinement of her hospital bed was to obey and be helpful to the nurses, take the medication prescribed, eat well, drink plenty of fluids, and try to keep in good spirits. The unsung heroes of Hospital Radio were a great help in that last task.

Where are you now? 23rd November 1977

Where are you now?
O child who cried for better things to come,
Who felt she lived in night when in the sun,
Where is she now?

Where are you now,
O child who chased the night to find the day,
Who lost herself while searching for the way,
Who kept her soul but threw her life away;
Where is she now?

Where are you now,
Oh child who stole my laughter and my time,
Who forgot reason while she chose the rhyme,
Who lost the world for something more sublime:
Where is she now?

    This simple reflection about the changes that occur as a person genuinely seeks a way out of depression, is more powerful taken out of its original context of a three-part poem written during a long hospital stay.
    Though the locusts stole many years, the transformation has given back four times as many better years. Yes, recovery is a long and challenging process, but its rewards make going through that change so worthwhile.

That's What It Takes   **August 1971**

That's what it takes –
Three black crosses on a windswept hill;
A grey sky with orange-red clouds,
The lights of the city behind –
That's what it takes.

That's what it takes –
A frightened walk on a path of stones
Through stark shadowed trees
Crying in the wind –
That's what it takes.

That's what it takes –
An unfailing trust in someone or something,
And a pledge to live that trust,
Whatever it costs –
That's what it takes.

Another of the poems Maggie wrote while a sixteen-year-old living in London. She believes her Christian faith must have protected her from the many real dangers around her. How hard her guardian angel must have worked to keep her safe until her return home!

That Fair Land of Peace reflects how, as a young person, Maggie never felt at home in the world she inhabited. At one point, she believed her life was the punishment for some heinous crime she had committed in another existence.

She wrote the poem in response to a homework assignment she had misunderstood while at school many years before. The paucity of her own efforts, in comparison with the beautiful writing of others in her class, kept rankling. Did that little piece of grit, years later, help her make a pearl?

It was to be many years before Maggie learned to let go of the past with its disappointments, and concentrate her energies on living in the present.

That Fair Land of Peace 30th March 1976

To take the flag, to fly – to wing
Across the ocean with the gulls;
To laugh and love, to hope and sing,
And drink a cup of life that's full
Of happiness and joyful things:
That's what I would my life me bring.

To take a boat, to sail to sea,
Across to other islands green;
To fight and win, and thereby be
In that fair land where all's serene –
That noble, powerful country
Where I am one with all that's free.

To take the road, to walk; to ride
Across the fells to other fields;
To clasp hands with you, by my side,
And sup the balm which all wounds heals;
And, forgetting past, hate and pride,
In that fair land of peace to bide.

The poet wrote *Lord Jesus walked this earth before* in the spring of the year that led to the start of a great transformation in her life.

In December 1983, Maggie volunteered to be secretary of the Thursday Group, a meeting of twelve men and women who gathered every fortnight from across West Cumbria and south Scotland, to pray for healing and spiritual growth, for the members, for others and for the world. One of the group presented the Twelve Step Program of Alcoholics Anonymous as a programme of living which could help people with other spiritual and emotional problems. Though Maggie joined the group to serve, she felt she was the one who gained the most from attending those meetings.

Lord Jesus walked this earth before   March 1983

Lord Jesus walked this earth before;
He walks beside us still:
He shares our sorrows and our joys
When we trust to His will;
But by ourselves we cannot live
According to His word;
So when each day we kneel and pray,
Ask, 'Guide me, please, O Lord.'

Lord Jesus walked this earth before;
He knows our mortal plight;
And he has shown the narrow way
To conquer Satan's might;
So when temptations sweetly call
And Satan's ploys applaud;
To Christ turn back in the attack
And pray, 'Forgive me, Lord.'

Lord Jesus walked this earth before;
He knows that we are weak:
The venal echoes of the world
Drown out the peace we seek;
But when distracted by its noise
Or by its wealth allured,
Pray, 'Come to me and set me free,
And bring me home, O Lord.'

Lord Jesus walked this earth before
And will return again
In might to set the captives free
And judge the fate of men.
We know not when that hour will be,
That hour of just reward;
So from now on we'll lean upon
The mercy of our Lord.

Had I known then is a poem of mature reflection. It compares the differences between our perceptions in childhood and adulthood. Resentments carried into adult life, are symptoms of the adult still thinking and acting as a child.

Through the Twelve Step Programme of recovery, Maggie identified those places where the inner child still controlled her emotions, and found ways to overcome that. One was to learn to love the child within her who had felt so helpless and unloved before. The simple meditation involved can be very helpful.

In your mind's eye, crouch down and open your arms to your childhood self. Give that child who was you all the cuddles and hugs you had needed then. Accept that child in all her or his completeness, not just those 'good' parts which had previously won approval.

Then review your relationship with your parents. Had they been damaged, too? Had they done the best they could in the circumstances they found themselves?

Through such techniques, Maggie learned to love her parents for themselves, rather than hold them guilty of denying her things they could not possibly have given. This altered attitude transformed their relationship, and the rest of their years together.

Had I known then   20th February 2023

That little girl cried herself to sleep so many nights.
The world seemed like a prison;
The sentence without reprieve.
She sought to leave so many times, but failed:
Yet another failure in the catalogue of despair.

We each believed our different childhoods were the norm,
That other homes were like ours;
That we all saw the same things.
Then, as we grew and went our separate ways,
Our ignorance and distance entrenched the myth.

I had to learn to love that little girl hiding inside
Who no-one else seemed to love.
I had to believe in her:
To cherish her for all her quirks and faults;
To have faith in all her hopes and dreams -
Those hopes and dreams which others had ignored.

This mature woman blossomed from that late loved child.
On firm foundations at last,
My eyes opened to the truths:
Most parents try to do the best they can;
And none of us are born equal in talent, time or place.

Had I known this then, how many tears could I have saved?
But could such a naïve child
Grasp such a complex concept?
To forgive my parents is not enough:
Now I give them my respect, which had been so long denied.

This gentle meditation follows the course of a river in a landscape from its spring in the hills, through the lowlands to the coast until it merges with the sea and returns to the skies.

We too can use the momentum of daily existence to draw us through life in that endless cycle of birth, death and rebirth. There may be times to strive against the flow, but there will also be times to relax and let the flow take us where it will.

How relaxing it can be to step out of our complex lives for a moment, to lie back and listen to the music of water flowing in a stream and the waves breaking upon a shore.

River   13th July 1975
                                                       7th February 2023

River, wind,
Wind down the hill
And lead me where
I'll find God's will.

River wind
Across the vale
And lead me where
I can prevail.

River wind
Down to the shore
And lead me where
I'll run no more.

River wind
Into the sea
And lead me where
I can be free.

River, wind
Until you rise
And join the clouds
Up in the skies.

Section Five

Stories

The Manson Affair Trilogy   July 1972

I

Travellers of the road, we're born;
Into Life's fast race we're thrown;
Never knowing, never known.

Fighters of the world by right;
Alien in each other's sight,
Each man an army in the fight.

Losers of the world by trade;
Searching sunshine, finding shade,
As past experiences fade...

Is there such a thing as love?
Can I believe in God above?
Surely life is far too tough.

Will I see tomorrow's sun?
Will I still be on the run?
And will I ever homeward come?

Get along the road, man –
We've gotta hit another load
Before they smash our code, man,
So you get along the road...

II

Lit by the starry heavens –
The light of times gone by –
Are floating orbs of magic
Covering the sky.

Drifting across the pathways
Created before all time
Are swirling mists of stars
Called "Travellers' Wine".

People are called by the stars –
Their lights beckon them on –
Never remembering
They can't go home.

III

Sun blaze,
Starry skies,
See the sadness in her eyes
As all the universe she spies.

Short age,
Flying time,
Makes light work of living's wine
As people's fortunes intertwine.

Barbed lies,
Spiked words
Cut much sharper than the sword
Goes through Life's shining silver cord.

Dawn hill,
Silent fool –
Death's for those who play it cool –
An angel's luck or Satan's fuel.

So play to win or you will fall,
For death's for those who play it cool.
So play to win,
And you'll win through.

The Manson Affair Trilogy and *What can a revolutionary do* were both inspired by the Zoe Manson series of science fiction novels, as yet unpublished. The dystopian view of superficial civilisation described in the novels has been edited out slightly in these two songs so that a British audience can make sense of their messages.

The series follows a young woman living in the twilight world between legitimate business and the black market, using her situation to help stateless people and refugees find a new home, employment and security.

What can a revolutionary do   **July 1972**

What can a revolutionary do
When you're a no-one?
What can you do
When you've got no home?

Take a room in the basement:
That's where we began.
Look around for others –
Find us if you can.

What can a revolutionary do
When you're on the breadline?
What can you do
When you can't see sunshine?

Make a home in the basement:
That's how we began.
Sign up for the social;
Find hope if you can.

What can a revolutionary do
When you're walking a tightrope?
What can you do
When you've got no hope?

Make some friends in the basement:
That's why we began.
There's no way out but the sewer,
So find peace if you can.

A rebel hero with a heart for the poor has always been a leading motif in much Maggie's writing. Her Christian faith and her father's socialism gave her a desire to defend the rights of those who cannot defend themselves. Her father could recall, in the 1920s to 1930s, families so poor, they had to steal turnips from his father's fields in order to eat. He described returning sheep to a sheep farm high in the West Lakeland moors, and facing a dilemma about accepting the farmer's hospitality. All the family had to eat were potatoes, and he did not want to deprive them of the little food they had.

This poem is a reflection about an archetypal saviour of the common people, who gave so generously that he lost everything he had to the cause. He is not a representation of Jesus, because he was married, he had an army and he was fighting abroad. The poem leaves the reader to decide whether the fight is physical or figurative and the foreign land a reference to the hostile environment in which he lived and worked.

But there is a powerful sense of the failure felt by his followers after his death. Could the disciple Jesus loved have lamented the events of Good Friday similarly, not realising the Easter transformation that would soon arrive?

To the unknown hero   26th June 1976

I saw the starving people peering through the bars,
Tearing at the heavy chains imprisoning their hearts;
I saw the crying children, ragged clothes and dirty hair,
And I heard their aged, hopeless cries…
                      then saw that you were there.

I saw you in that prison cell, where you were working truth,
While I sang beauty's dirges, and you smiled at my youth –
Then I saw the ray of sunshine, I saw the promised hope
Which helped me from the mine's deep shaft
                      upon its golden rope.

Brothers, sisters joined you as you tried to save our lives,
Easing tired and aching souls with a balm so long denied.
I saw you with your army, fighting in that foreign land;
Then just one bullet stopped you – and no-one was at hand.

You gave yourself so freely, they took everything you had.
They laughed and stole your money, but still your heart was glad;
So they took away your reason, and they took away your wife,
And when they'd finished with your workings,
                      they took away your life.

And we were your fighters,
We were your army,
We were your disciples –
Where are your soldiers now?

Interlude is an example of Maggie's creative ramblings as she fleshes out the characters of people in her novels. This poem describes a possible conversation between Liz Kirkland and her friend Bethany Broome, before Liz sobered up and became the heroine of the two *Diviner's Nemesis* novels, available at www.eregendal.com/books.

Interlude   17th June 1975

Bethany threw a handful of coins in the air.
'We don't want to know yes or no – we want to know the possibilities,' she said, moving them across the floor.
Outside, it was raining, and the bushes were glistening in the watery moonlight.
My thoughts were far away.

There is a star in the heavens
That lights the way
To the daylight;
And though I know
It is midnight,
Yet here I will stay.

There is a hope in the heavens
That shines on me
In my dream time;
And though I know
I'm drunk with wine,
Yet here will I be.

There is a path in the heavens
That calls my name
With that same call…
And though I know
I may well fall,
Yet here I'll remain.

'Were you listening?' Bethany asked.
'What?' I stammered shyly.
'Never mind. I only said it was fifty-fifty.'

Little Peter   30th March 1975

Little Peter,
They can't see that you are laughing, laughing
Why do you not drop your mask and cry?
Oh, little Peter,
They can't know that you are sneering, sneering.
Why do you not bare your breast and try?

They told me you were leaving on the train –
They told me you would not be back again.
Oh, little Peter, why don't you cry?
Oh, little Peter, why don't you try?

Little Peter,
They can't see that all you are is acting, acting.
Why don't you take your make-up off and cry?
Oh, little Peter,
They can't know that you are lonely, lonely.
Why don't you draw the curtains and try?

They told me you were leaving on the train –
They told me you would not be back again.
Oh, little Peter, why don't you cry?
Oh, little Peter, why don't you try?

Snap!
There was a truth, a youth, but now he's gone.
There was a dream, a scheme, but now he's alone.
Snap!

We listened.
The train drew alongside the platform.
We watched.
Little Peter opened the door and threw in his case.

We waited.
A face appeared at a window and smiled.
We waved.
A pale blue handkerchief floated to our motionless feet.
We turned.
The train sang a duet with the rails as it pulled away.
We cried.

Oh, little Peter,
They never knew that underneath you mourned, mourned,
For you never dropped your mask and cried.
Oh, little Peter,
They never knew that within their walls your heart died, died,
For you never bared your breast and tried.

I watched you, with them, leaving on the train –
I knew with them, you'd not be back again.
Oh, little Peter, why did you never cry?
Oh, little Peter, why did you never try?

This story song came to Maggie without planning as she put pen to paper. It appears to have emerged from her own decision to run away five years prior to the poem being written. It clearly describes the confusion of emotions and the masking that are so common with people on the autistic spectrum.

Ginny Lee   May 1975

Smile for me, Ginny Lee:
When the day is not enough,
Laugh for me,
Smile for me,
Sadly Ginny Lee.

Cry for me, Ginny Lee,
When the gloomy night is nigh,
Sign for me,
Cry for me,
Lonely Ginny Lee.

Think of me, Ginny Lee,
When memories are all we keep,
Dream of me,
Think of me,
Happy Ginny Lee.

Ginny Lee was one of the three main characters in *The Three Circled Star*, yet to be published. The poet wrote the section about the character Ginny Lee much earlier than the rest of the book. Too short to stand alone, it stayed in a file until Maggie developed a reasonable plot to flesh out the rest of the novel.

Ginny suffered from mental health problems, which made her come across as both selfish and very vulnerable. Others exploited that vulnerability.

Ghost Story   11ᵗʰ May 2021

I loved to play my forbidden flute
to the trees and the beasts of the forest,
to the stream and the fish of the waters,
standing among them on the craggy rock.

And since I fell from that rock into that stream,
I can play there forever,
weaving my haunting tunes
through the dappled noises of the woods,
calling all creatures to rejoice.

I'm free of the rules that stopped me
living as a child in life.
Now I live as Pan,
calling you to join with me
in the cosmic dance of joy
that sings in all creation.

Ghost Story was the product of a writing exercise set during the Nottingham Beyond the Spectrum course in 2021. The course helped creative autists explore different writing techniques in poetry and prose in a safe environment.

The object of this exercise was to create a short poem from the large back story each participant had created through answering a series of questions posed by the course leader.

Anya was a character in *The Eagle and The Butterfly*, the closest friend of the narrating character Eregendal. When they meet again after six years, Eregendal helps Anya find a way through her depression. In return, Anya invites Eregendal on an expedition to find the Tree of Knowledge at the top of the world, a life-changing experience for all who took part.

The Eagle and The Butterfly is available from www.eregendal.com/books.

To Anya, The Second Song   3rd December 1977

And others sleep,
While in the distance this star burns
Which burned so oft before.

And others dream,
While in the shadows this heart cries
Which cried so oft before.

And others rise,
While in the evening this sun sets
Which set so oft before.

And others sing,
While in the twilight this mind mourns
Which mourned so oft before.

And others live,
While in the midnight this soul dies,
Which died so oft before.

By Inspiration 11ᵗʰ June 1975

And she lifts a hand of wonder
To the citizens of the deep,
For she thinks that they've an answer
To the crop that she must reap;
    While she waves a flag of surrender
    From the highest turret walls;
    But no consent is brought her
    And so empty, the flag falls.
So she sings a song of sorrow
That she'd written to the light,
A sad song of tomorrow…
But I only have tonight.

Casting petals on the castle moat
She looked across the fell
And watched the lazy seagulls float
In the hazy summer spell.
    And she listened to my ramblings
    About Death and Light and Truth,
    And she said I could not see things
    Being blinded by my youth.
Now she sings a song of sorrow
That she'd written to her light –
A sad song for tomorrow –
But I only have tonight.

For she cannot see the sunrise,
In the depths of my dark eyes,
And though she looks across my skies,
She cannot see my many lies.
    And I was lost inside her mind
    Because I found that I was blind
    When I had thought that I could see –
    But that was just the other me.

So she sings a song of sorrow
That she'd written in the light:
A sad song for tomorrow –
But I only have tonight.

For the castle walls and tenement slums
Are crumbling to the earth,
All overfilled with sluts and bums
Who have no gratitude for birth.
    And the night is killed by neon
    And the day locked out by blinds;
    And the hearts of men die in their towns –
Too selfish to be kind.

So I sing a song of sorrow
Which has never seen the light,
Nor will it see tomorrow
For I only have tonight.
    For I am lost inside her mind,
    Just having found that I was blind
    When I had thought that I could see –
    But that's because the she was me.

    This was an early description of Tamara in *The Eagle and The Butterfly*, developing her character as an insensitive mentor.
    Tamara was the archetype for creative inspiration: beautiful, cruel, demanding, unpredictable, and expecting total obedience.

Escape   1st June 1975
                                             16th February 2023

There's nothing much to look forward to these days.
An empty purse and not enough to go round.
The wood-built farmstead feels chilly and grey:
Apart from the moaning wind, there is no sound.

Outside on the veranda, Joe sits and dreams
With work-boot feet up on the paint-chipped railings
And a lazy heart that's full of wild schemes
Of what he'd do with the time and other things.

Across the windswept fields, the boys break their backs,
While red cattle browse among black sheep who lie,
And rooks shriek angry cackles of alarm
When the storm prevents them taking to the sky.

Meanwhile, in the seclusion of my small room,
The mirror I look into, looks into me;
We stare each other out across the gloom,
Waiting for the menfolk's ninetieth cup of tea.

Shadowed image on the wall, what knows you now?
Gaunt cheeks, sunken face, emaciated smile –
Nothing but rags and skin and bone below,
And a genteel voice which once betokened style.

Tired and reddened eyes that gaze through stinging tears;
Pitted hands and forehead, burnt brown in the sun;
Greying unwashed hair bleached by all the years
Spent fearfully hiding, keeping on the run.

In the darkened street at midnight
Came five men to do you down.
Since then, five years of half light
Shifting from town to town.

But shadows aren't a woman's friend,
Nor can the chameleon's coat forever hide...
Tired eyes, is it that you see the end,
Or do you see the end denied?

This poem about escape has a haunted feel to it. The woman running from her past, has begun to realise how much she lost by failing to confront the danger she had once fled from rather than face. Does she now need to escape from that escape?

Section Six

People and Places

This light-hearted song is a throw-back to the pop songs of the 1960s, recalling a more innocent era when teenagers left home to work in the city, living in bedsits until 'The One' finally came along to rescue them.

I Don't Love You, Boy April 1979

Last night I sat at home,
Thinking of you,
Where had you gone?
I looked for your car –
It wasn't there.
Listening at my window,
Dreaming all alone.
No, I don't love you, boy,
But I miss you when you're gone.

Each time we meet,
Out in the hall,
Down in the street,
I try to catch your eye,
Say hello.
Then I start to speak
But my words come out all wrong.
No, I don't love you, boy,
But I'm shy when we're alone.

Don't you remember me?
I'm the lonely girl
In room number 3.
I wait for your knock
Every day.
Maybe we could talk,
Get to know each other more.
Guess I might just love you, boy:
Let's find out when you come through my door.

This traditional poem and song is a sad reflection on a fading relationship, told through the medium of walking in different landscapes, one of the poet's favourite motifs.

Emptiness in Cumbria   23rd January 1975

I walk on the strand by the sullen sea
And hear the gulls call as they cry to me
And wish I had wings to fly so free –
For I love the sea and the wind's cold roar
But I love thee no more.

I climb the steel fell and look down on the lake
And wish its calm depths my mind could take
For regret weighs my thoughts and makes my heart ache;
Still, I love the sea and the wind's cold roar
But I love thee no more.

I sit by the beck on a weather-worn rock
Taunted by its free waters which cruelly mock,
For I'm jailed in a prison that I can't unlock.
Still, I love the sea and the wind's cold roar
But I love thee no more.

I stroll between trees in the gloomy wood
And hear the tops soughing in tune with my mood:
Their symphonies ease my soul as I brood;
For I love the sea and the wind's cold roar
But I love thee no more.

The wind tugs my coat and ruffles my hair:
To face tempests alone and to walk to nowhere
Is far better for me than to face you there.
For I love the sea and the wind's cold roar,
But I love thee no more.

Independence is a poem about a claustrophobic relationship where one longs to keep their freedom and yet also feels tempted to succumb to the other's pressure to become more intimate.

It can be hard to maintain one's personal boundaries when one is reliant on someone else's generosity, as the poet was when she wrote this poem.

Independence   21st December 1977

You hold me in your claws, friend –
I feel your grip tightening
And I am fearful.

Yet it is tempting to relax,
To fall into your cushioned trap,
To stop fighting.

But what if I then turn,
Turn to flee the cage,
Only to be barred?

No, let me fight for my independence,
Let me stretch my wings still:
Leave me to fly.

Patient bulldog, you can wait,
For we both see the future inevitable,
Though now I struggle.

Let me tire myself out roaming the fells:
My tired wings will bring me home more surely
Than if you clipped them.

Let me come home in my own time.
For all your chains, you will keep me
Safer when I'm free.

Tim Hardin wrote the classic songs *If I Were A Carpenter* and *Reason to Believe*, both of which Maggie admired greatly and liked to sing herself. His appearance at Whitehaven Civic Hall in 1975 was unexpected. She went with friends to see him perform. Before the concert started, they spotted the singer in the bar at the back of the hall, getting drinks in before he went on stage. He died of a heroin overdose five years later, in December 1980.

Maggie wrote this poem soon after his performance in Whitehaven.

To Tim Harding: A Reflection   5th July 1975

A dead mouse lies out in the back yard;
A trapped bird flutters desperately against the window;
Remains of yesterday lie strewn around,
In the shadow of a half-full wine bottle.

The cat's paw pounces, feathers flutter to the floor,
And a fake Grecian urn lies shattered on the sill.
Water slowly drips, patting on the tiles;
But unseeing eyes observe it kiss the ground.

Unseeing eyes, you rule a stranger's face,
A face of time and tears, of past laughter and past love;
Stroked by hands marked by the string and the pen,
Feeling into the body for the works of the mind.

Lost and lonely singer, why rest you here,
When you have another pittance show to play,
Another chord to practise, another song to write –
Have you the time or money just to sit and wait?

"The half-full bottle of wine will be empty tonight,
And yesterday will be tomorrow's today;
For I am the trapped bird
           fluttering desperately against the window,
And the dead mouse is the hope and force of my soul."

Nightmare City   3rd August 1975

Nightmare city, I'm leaving you behind:
Your day-lit night, your smiles unkind –
Pushing your memory to the back of my mind.
Oh! Goodbye, old home town.

Nightmare city, I'm hurrying away
From your chaos, your madness, your sickening decay.
Could I stand your fight just one more day?
No! Goodbye, old home town.

Nightmare city, you don't really care
If I stay with you or leave for anywhere.
I hear your voices, filled with despair.
So goodbye, old home town.

Nightmare city, you know I'll be back:
Your sad song haunts me down this rocky track.
How I wish I'd never seen your heart of black.
So goodbye, old home town.

    Nightmare City and *I can't quit you* were both inspired by the Zoe Manson series of novels, and also the poet's dislike of living in cities for any longer than necessary.
    The blues song *I can't quit you* has a strong walking bass typical of its genre. Maggie has performed the song in public several times. She has never performed *Nightmare City* live though, after realising the long foreboding introduction was an unconscious copy of similar walking bass riffs by the Beatles and Yes.

I Can't Quit You
September 1973
1st April 1976

I can't quit those bright, bright lights
Though they blind me inside.
No, I can't quit your bright bright lights,
Though they make me wanna hide.
I might try to run away in fear,
But those damn lights always drag me back here.
Oh, I can't quit you, sad old town.

I can't quit those great, great crowds
Though they make me hide away.
No, I can't quit your great great crowds
Though they trap me night and day.
I might try to cover up my face,
But those damn crowds still force me to this place.
Oh, I can't quit you, bad old town.

I can't quit those tall, tall towers
Though they stop me seeing the skies.
No, I can't quit your tall tall towers,
Though they crush me with their size.
I might try to bury myself away
But those damn towers somehow get me out each day.
Oh, I can't quit you, sad old town.

I can't quit those broad, broad streets,
Though the cars would run me down.
No, I can't quit your broad broad streets
Though I'm deafened by their sounds.
I might try to leave the beaten track
But those damn streets always lead me back
Oh, I can't quit you, bad old town.

Kid   **1971**

Kid, you're a damn' bloody fool,
And you know it:
You've put your foot in it this time,
And you show it.

Kid, I prayed for you when they came to get you –
They didn't get you.
Don't you show your face in here again!
I won't let you.

Kid, surely you know where you went wrong -
I could tell you.
Just go away and don't come back no more -
I won't sell you.

Kid, we all go wrong in life sometimes -
You just took the trump card.
Hell, your Dadda and me was worse than you -
You just fell too hard.

Kid, go on your way with our blessing -
Remember us.
I know you'll make it someday.
Pray for us.

Kid, I'll miss you…
Christ, how I'll miss you…

15 lines to the bottle of wine   23rd September 1974

What colour is the sky, my child?
The sky is bright, the sky is blue:
I search its depths for something new.

What colour is the sky, my friend?
The sky is dull, the sky is grey
With memories of yesterday.

What colour is the sky, mother?
The sky is deep, the sky is red:
I see the sunset up ahead.

What colour is the sky, old man?
The sky is naught, the sun is cold:
Our time is done, we are both old.

What colour is the sky? To me
The sky is dark and black as night.
I don't know when I last saw light.

The poet wrote the poignant poem *Rover*, when she was fourteen. Its description of the life of a vagrant shows she was already thinking about leaving home, long before she succeeded the following May.

Rover   August 1969

I'm a rover:
With the wild winds and the rushing seas I roam.
I'm a loner,
And there's no-one there to comfort me as I roam.

When the sun dies,
You can hear my footsteps echo through the skies.
When the rain falls
You can hear my laughter echo through the hills.

Crowded cities
Tend to spurn my freedom of the open road.
Full of pity,
I pass by those blinkered people and their goals.

With the birdsong,
My heart seeks the empty valleys and the seas,
And the bright sun
Tends to shine on me as I lead a life that's free.

But take me back to the place I miss:
I remember it so well still.
Which is home? That or this?
For I still roam, against my will.

But I'm a rover:
With the wild winds and the rushing seas I roam.
I'm a loner,
And there's no-one there to comfort me as I roam.

The curious poem, *Sassechusas Mary*, describes a relationship between two friends, where one is manipulating the other, who had not learned to set enough boundaries to prevent being abused.

Autistic children are often taught that their boundaries don't matter, in situations where neurotypical people want them to behave like neurotypical people, too. In adulthood, that learned behaviour leaves autists open to having their rights abused. It is important for autists to learn as young adults how to set boundaries in relationships, trusting that their maintaining boundaries will not automatically make the other person dislike them.

The place name Sassechusas was an invention created for its rhythm.

Sassechusas Mary   30th March 1975

Sassechusas Mary, where have you been?
You left the house and washing once again!
You took your heart and left it in the rain
Because you never want to love again.

Sassechusas Mary, what do you see?
Why did you want to laugh and toy with me?
You took my hand and led me to the sea
Because you thought you felt something for me.

Sassechusas Mary, why do you cry?
You walked the ocean strand and sought the sky,
And took my empty dreams and made them lie
Because you wanted me to hear you sigh.

Sassechusas Mary, where have you been?
You broke your heart and my heart once again:
You wrecked my world and drowned me in your dream –
Yet now you say *you'll* never love again!

The evocative song, *Milestone to Peace*, was inspired by the stories and artwork of the artist Heather Bolton RA, who journeyed with a friend in a minivan from Great Britain to Pakistan in the late 1960s. The song is a reflection about the landscape passed on the road to Bamyan while crossing Afghanistan.

Milestone to Peace   4th February 1976

Milestone to peace: yours is no easy way –
The ancient rugged rocks affray
All who walk your way.

Milestone to peace: yours is no easy path –
Crowding mountains still the laugh
Of those on the path.

Milestone to peace, yours is no easy road –
Sinister moonlit cliffs forebode
Ill on Pilgrims Road.

Milestone to peace: yours is no easy route –
You stand black in the vale of doubt,
Trapped seer by the route.

Milestone to peace: yours is no easy track –
Yet here I stand: I can't go back –
Nor walk on along your track.

Section Seven

Humour

This oddity came to the poet out of nowhere one day. It reads as if a local gossip is sinking their claws deeply into other people in their community. The last verse tells the reader it is all a lie anyway, which is often the case with gossip.

Fry La Dame Porte Cable   16th May 1975

His name's Madame Cherchez La Porte.
People call him Churchie for short
Because he always gives no thought
To all the things he really ought
While seeking the things he's always sought,
Which can be sold, but can't be bought.

Her name's Monsieur Fifi La Dame
Because, it is said, she's always game,
Rarely has enough, and never is tame
Especially considering matters of fame
(Or at least the people who from that shrine came)
And excels herself putting them all to shame.

Your name's Josephine Benjamin Cable,
Reputedly clever and even more able
At giving the people around you a label
For being bedecked in suit, rags or sable,
While dining in parks or at the high table,
So that you can condemn them to dying in Babel.

My name's Jonathan Angela Fry –
A person pretending to look at the sky
While really regarding all those who pass by
Who all think they're so much greater than I
And don't know I'm much greater when I try –
Except I don't bother because I am shy.

In 1972, the poet worked as a temporary clerk helping to merge two filing systems of poems and captions after Kays Cards took over Forget Me Not Cards.

During her lunch breaks, Maggie wrote several greetings cards spoofs, some of which her fellow clerks filed into the new system. One wonders how the firm's artists would illustrate these verses.

Greeting Card Pastiches   Summer 1972

You're the sugar in my sweetheart;
You're the pastry in my pie;
And if you go on like this, mate,
Then you're nuttier than I!!

If I had a custard pie,
Do you know what I'd do?
I'd stand up tall,
And take good aim,
And throw it over you!

This little kitty's come to say
She's sorry 'bout the poo,
But she's just "shitted" on the mat
Cos she just can't stand you!

I sure hope Santa's got some
    Goodies for you
Cos I will want
    To use them too.
Jewellery, sports cars,
    Cash and clobber,
I'll take them - Signed:
    Your local robber.

And the cause of
    All this riddle?
Yes, mates!
    We're all on the
        "Fiddle"!!

Biking Song was inspired by a bike ride the poet made across London from Wimbledon to Elstree in a couple of hours in June 1972. The next day, she cycled back again. Fortunately, her rides were not quite so full of incident as the journey in this light-hearted song.

Biking song   June 1972

Chorus: Pedalling over to you,
          I'm pedalling over to you,
          Pedalling over to you, boy,
          I'm pedalling over to you.

Hadn't gone but a quarter mile
When bang went my gear two,
But I just didn't stop pedalling cos
I'm pedalling over to you.

Hadn't gone but five miles on
When I came to a traffic queue,
But I just found me another route
While pedalling over to you.

Hadn't gone but ten miles on
When I saw a wonderful view,
But I just took me a snap-shot cos
I'm pedalling over to you.

Hadn't gone but seven miles on
When I stopped for a cup of quick brew,
But I never stopped at that place long
Cos I needed to use your loo.

Great rejoicing two miles on
Cos I had finally got through,
And I collapsed in my lover's arms
Cos I've pedalled over to you.

Last Chorus: I've pedalled over to you,
              I've pedalled over to you,
              I've pedalled over to you, boy,
              I've pedalled over to you!

What did I do?   1st August 1983

What, what did I do
To deserve someone like you?
You came right out of the blue:
There was nothing that I could do.
I thought I was fine –
I must have been right out of my mind
To think my dreams could come true.
Tell me, what can I do?

In 1983, the poet had the brilliant idea of writing a musical which would be so fabulous it would make her an overnight sensation. She wrote several songs for it, 'each sadly even more pathetic than the last,' she later confessed. This is one that continues to stick in the memory, despite all attempts to dislodge it.

And finally…

When I was young   **May 1975**

When I was young
My mother said
That I should sleep
Alone in bed.
This rule I never
Would ignore,
And so we do it
On the floor.

Thank you for buying this book. If you have enjoyed these poems, please leave a review at the online bookstore where you made your purchase or on our website, www.eregendal.com using the QR code below.

We read and appreciate every one.

About the Author

Author Maggie Shaw creates her stories from her many and varied life experiences. A teenage runaway who made good before her autistic spectrum disorder diagnosis, Maggie writes as one who has walked the walk in recovery and spiritual development. Her degrees in science, divinity and church music, and her career as a Mental Health Dietitian, give a solid framework to the exciting adventure stories she loves to tell. The Scottish hills and Lakeland fells where her forebears farmed often feature as landscapes in her work.

Maggie is also a church musician, composer and songwriter, and many of her songs are inspired by the stories she writes.

This is the ninth book Maggie has published through micropublisher Eregendal. Her music and short stories have been broadcast by Radio Carlisle, Cat Radio, and Red Shift Radio; and she has contributed articles to The St Raphael's Guild *Chrism*, The Church of England Newspaper, and *Soul and Spirit* Magazine. Online, Maggie publishes through ArtSwarm, YouTube, SoundCloud, Facebook and the Eregendal website www.eregendal.com.

Maggie lives in Cheshire with her husband Alan and their cat, Tarby.

Index of Poems

15 lines to the bottle of wine	105
Biking Song	119
Black Candle	45
By Inspiration	88
Circles	52
Emptiness in Cumbria	97
Escape	90
Fly Away	43
For All Eternity	11
Fry La Dame Porte Cable	115
Ghost Story	85
Ginny Lee	84
Greeting Card Pastiches	117
Had I known then	69
How I Miss You	21
I Can't Quit You	103
I Don't Love You, Boy	95
Independence	99
Interlude	81
It sure is a hard world, man, but…	32
Just four more little months	31
Just Say The Word	13
Kid	104
Like a shadow, the night	47
Little Peter	82
Look on and Laugh	23
Lord Jesus walked this earth before	66
Love Song	15
Milestone to Peace	111
My Love	12
Nightmare City	102

Index of Poems - continued

Now We Rest	37
Numbers	29
Pattern	19
Prisoner	60
Raise your glass	61
River	71
Rover	107
Sassechusas Mary	109
Selah, Selah	59
Starshine	42
That Fair Land of Peace	65
That's What It Takes	63
The aftermath of sorrow	55
The Last Song	39
The Manson Affair Trilogy	74
The Night Watchman	33
The Unseen Castle	50
To Anya, The Second Song	87
To Dying Love	17
To my psychiatrist	48
To the unknown hero	79
To Tim Hardin: A Reflection	101
Twixt Sky and Sod	54
Untitled	52
What can a revolutionary do	77
What did I do?	120
When I was young	121
When I…	27
When it's all over	53
Where are you now?	62
Where is the scheme	20
Why Cry 'Blood'?	35

www.ingramcontent.com/pod-product-compliance
Lightning Source LLC
LaVergne TN
LVHW021355080426
835508LV00020B/2290